394.2695
195
HO

Ho, Siow Yen.

South Korea

77916

$16.95

DATE DUE	BORROWER'S NAME	ROOM NO.

T 77916

394.2695
195
HO

Ho, Siow Yen.

South Korea

Festivals *of the* World

SOUTH KOREA

Gareth Stevens Publishing
MILWAUKEE

Written by
HO SIOW YEN

Edited by
AUDREY LIM

Designed by
HASNAH MOHD ESA

Picture research by
SUSAN JANE MANUEL

First published in North America in 1998 by
Gareth Stevens Publishing
1555 North RiverCenter Drive, Suite 201
Milwaukee, Wisconsin 53212 USA

For a free color catalog describing Gareth
Stevens' list of high-quality books and multimedia
programs, call
1-800-542-2595 (USA)
or 1-800-461-9120 (Canada).
Gareth Stevens Publishing's Fax: (414) 225-0377.
See our catalog, too, on the World Wide Web:
http://gsinc.com

© TIMES EDITIONS PTE LTD 1998
Originated and designed by
Times Books International
an imprint of Times Editions Pte Ltd
Times Centre, 1 New Industrial Road
Singapore 536196
Printed in Singapore

Library of Congress Cataloging-in-Publication Data:
Ho, Siow Yen.
South Korea / by Ho Siow Yen.
p. cm.—(Festivals of the world)
Includes bibliographical references and index.
Summary: Describes how the culture of South
Korea is reflected in its many festivals including
Lunar New Year, Buddha's Birthday, and National
Foundation Day.
ISBN 0-8368-2019-3 (lib. bdg.)
1. Festivals—Korea (South)—Juvenile literature. 2.
Korea (South)—Social life and customs—Juvenile
literature. [1. Festivals—Korea (South) 2.
Holidays—Korea (South) 3. Korea (South)—Social
life and customs.] I. Title. II. Series.
GT4886.K6R3 1998
394.2695195—dc21   97-52124

1 2 3 4 5 6 7 8 9 02 01 00 99 98

CONTENTS

It's Festival Time . . .

The Korean word for "festival" is *je* [jhe]. Some festivals celebrated in South Korea are similar to the festivals found in neighboring countries. However, throughout the centuries, South Koreans have celebrated their festivals in a unique way. So, come catch a glimpse of the moon, see women playing on swings, and watch colorful lantern parades go by. It's je time in South Korea...

3

WHERE'S SOUTH KOREA?

The Korean peninsula lies below China and Russia. It is surrounded by the Korea Strait to the south, the Sea of Japan to the east, and Korea Bay and the Yellow Sea to the

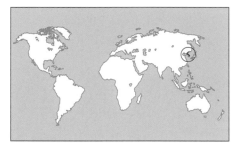

west. The "**Ceasefire Line**" divides the Korean peninsula into South Korea and North Korea. South Korea lies below this line. In the past, the whole of Korea was called *Choson* [CHO-sawn], meaning "The Land of the Morning Calm."

Who are the South Koreans?

A long time ago, wandering tribes of hunters, fishermen, and farmers entered Korea. These settlers created three kingdoms, which were eventually united to form Korea. Korea was ruled by different kings and was peaceful. However, it was **ravaged** by war when foreigners tried to conquer it for themselves. Korea therefore avoided the rest of the world and was called the Hermit Kingdom. After the second World War, Korea was divided into North and South Korea. Later, the **Korean War** (1950-1953) set the borders of the present North and South Korea. The people living in South Korea are South Koreans.

A South Korean boy perched on the shoulders of an adult.

4

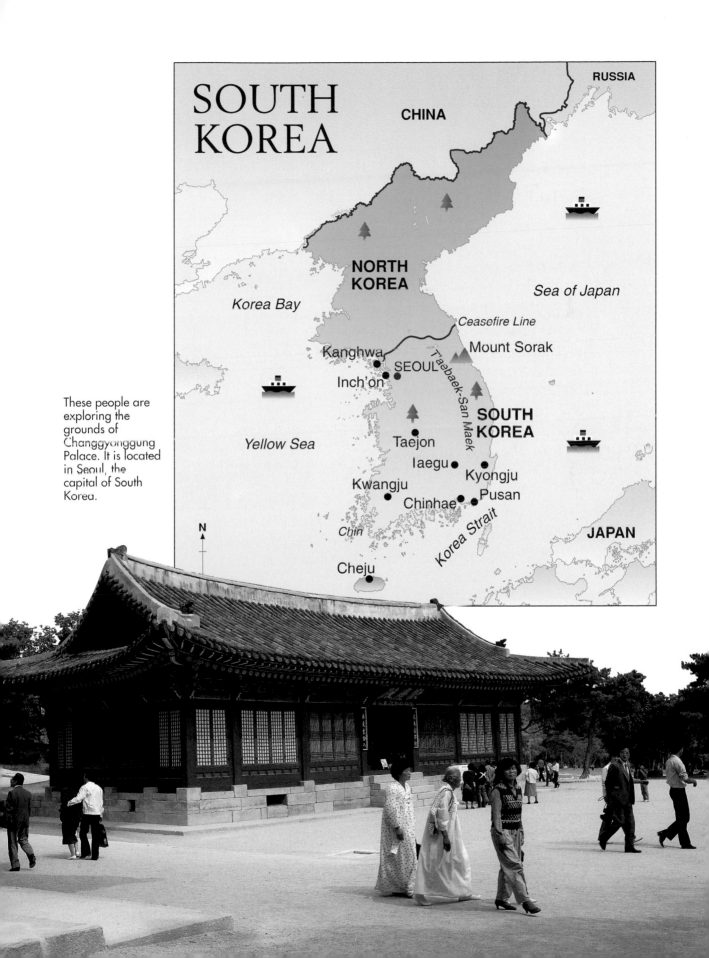

SOUTH KOREA

RUSSIA

CHINA

NORTH KOREA

Korea Bay

Sea of Japan

Ceasefire Line

Kanghwa

Mount Sorak

SEOUL

Inch'on

Taebaek-San Maek

SOUTH KOREA

Yellow Sea

Taejon

Iaegu

Kyongju

Kwangju

Pusan

Chinhae

Chin

Korea Strait

JAPAN

N

Cheju

These people are exploring the grounds of Changgyonggung Palace. It is located in Seoul, the capital of South Korea.

WHEN'S THE JE?

WINTER

⊛ **KIMJANG**—As winter approaches, Koreans make enough *kimchi* [KIM-chee] to last throughout the cold months ahead. Kimchi is a spicy, pickled vegetable dish. This tradition is practiced because people cannot buy the ingredients for kimchi during winter. People prepare kimchi and store it in crockery. These pots are buried up to their necks in the yard. During this time, the favorite greeting among housewives is "Have you finished *Kimjang* [KIM-jang]?"

Turn the pages and see what we do on Tan-O Day!

South Korean festivals are fun! Turn the pages and you'll see!

⊛ **LUNAR NEW YEAR** (1st day of 1st month)
⊛ **TAE-BO-RUM (THE GREAT MOON FESTIVAL)**—People gather on a hill and wait for the moon. Koreans believe that catching a glimpse of the first full moon as it rises will bring good luck for the coming year. They carry torches up the hill to welcome the rising moon. Those who are late for the moon's appearance still make wishes for the coming year.

SPRING

- ⊛ **BUDDHA'S BIRTHDAY** (8th day of 4th month)
- ⊛ **CHINHAE CHERRY BLOSSOM FESTIVAL**—Cherry blossoms bloom during spring. Korean families go outdoors to enjoy the weather and view the cherry trees. There are also sports contests and traditional music performances.
- ⊛ **KING TANJONG FESTIVAL**—A ceremony to remember the murdered boy-king, Tanjong, and his loyal officials who refused to serve the new king. There are fancy dress parades and Chinese poetry contests. Korean classical music is also played.
- ⊛ **CH'UN-HYANG FESTIVAL**—Held in honor of Ch'un-hyang, a heroine in a Korean love story. Separated from her husband, Ch'un-hyang ignored the advances of a governor. Her husband returned, and they lived happily ever after. During the festival, beauty contests are held. The story of Ch'un-hyang is also told.
- ⊛ **ARBOR DAY**—A day for reforestation. Trees are planted on this day.
- ⊛ **SOKCHONJE RITES** (1st day of 2nd month)

SUMMER

- ⊛ **TAN-O DAY** (5th day of 5th month)
- ⊛ **SOKCHONJE RITES** (Yes, again!) (1st day of 8th month)

AUTUMN

- ⊛ **CH'USOK DAY** (15th day of 8th month).
- ⊛ **TAN-GUN DAY, OR NATIONAL FOUNDATION DAY**—Commemorates the traditional founding of Korea by Tan-gun. Memorial ceremonies honor the legendary figure.

7

NEW YEAR'S DAY

For South Koreans, New Year's Day falls on two dates. It occurs on January 1st on the Gregorian calendar. People living in the city usually celebrate New Year's Day on this date. New Year's Day also falls on the first day of the first month on the lunar calendar. The first three days of the Lunar New Year are called *sol-nal* [SOL-nal]. These first three days are observed mostly by people living in the countryside. Although people in the countryside and the city celebrate New Year's Day on different days, they follow the same practices. Everybody wears new clothes and visits family and friends.

These two children are ready to visit their relatives. They're all dressed up in new clothes.

Clear the cobwebs and settle your bills

No matter which day is chosen for the celebrations, preparations are needed. Houses are cleaned and tidied. Old debts are repaid. Koreans believe it is dishonorable to bring old debts into the new year. The family will also enjoy a feast. On New Year's Day, people observe memorial services for their dead ancestors. Wearing their new clothes, they bow deeply, offering incense and food.

Take a deep bow

After the memorial ceremonies in the morning, children make
formal bows to their parents. In this way, children show how
grateful they are to their parents for taking care of them. This is
known as **filial piety**. Filial piety is very important in Korean culture.
Koreans think this quality is important in shaping a person's
character. On New Year's Day, it is therefore a custom to pay
respect to one's parents by bowing deeply.

New Year's Day is also a time to show respect for elders. People
visit grandparents and other relatives who are older than they are.
After bowing, they will receive gifts and words of advice from their
elders. Then they go around visiting friends and neighbors.

Tae-bo-rum

Fifteen days after the Lunar New Year, the first full moon appears on the horizon. People celebrate this event with songs and dances. In the past, the Korean New Year festivities ended on Tae-bo-rum [TAE-bo-rum].

Bridge walking

Folklore has it that a person who walks across a bridge on the night of Tae-bo-rum will be free from foot pains for that year. Anybody who walks across 12 bridges that night will be free from bad luck. It is no wonder that bridges are always creaking with footsteps on Tae-bo-rum!

Below: One game that South Koreans play on New Year's Day is *Yut* [yud]. Players throw four sticks into the air. When they land, the players get a number. This number tells each player how many spaces he or she can move a token around a playing board. The winner is the first to finish moving around the board.

Above: Koreans also like to fly kites on New Year's Day. Sometimes, people compete with each other in kite-flying contests.

Friendly fights and war games

On Tae-bo-rum, neighboring villages engage in big competitions. These competitions may seem serious but are all done in the name of good fun.

One of the games is a **mock** torch fight. Neighboring villages send boys and men into an open space. When the moon rises, the gong starting the game sounds. These people run toward their opponents with burning bundles of straw and wild weed. People rarely get injured in the torch fights. However, contestants usually get their clothes torn and their hair burned!

Tugs-of-war are held on Tae-bo-rum. These are lots of fun, and many villagers take part. People believe the winning village will enjoy good luck and good harvests. Everybody shouts and exerts full strength in the tug-of-war!

Think about this

South Korea is not the only country whose festivals are based on the lunar calendar. Israel officially follows the Gregorian calendar, but its holidays are set to the lunar calendar. This is because the lunar calendar is the calendar used in the Bible. Even the Islamic calendar is based on the moon!

On New Year's Day, people also enjoy a game called *chujon-nori* [CHA-jon-NO-ri]. Two wooden vehicles are placed where their tops can meet. Two people riding on top try to push each other down. At ground level, groups of people push and steer the vehicles. It is a very exciting game!

BUDDHA'S BIRTHDAY

On the eighth day of the fourth lunar month, Buddhists in South Korea celebrate Buddha's birthday. Devout Buddhists attend the many religious ceremonies held at temples. They offer prayers and hope for Buddha's blessings. How else do South Koreans celebrate this special occasion? Read on and find out!

Look at these long rows of lanterns just waiting to be lit for the parade!

The lantern parade has many eager participants. These two boys are raring to go!

Feast of the lanterns

Colorful paper lanterns **adorn** Buddhist temples on this day. In the evening, a lantern parade is held. All the lanterns in the temple and its courtyard are lit, offering a spectacular sight. There are also lantern processions on the streets where families bring their lanterns and walk down the streets. The lantern parade is a very important aspect of this day. People look forward to seeing the hundreds of candle lights flickering in the darkness. The lights within the lanterns symbolize hope. In fact, the lantern parade is so essential to the festival that Buddha's birthday is also called Feast of the Lanterns.

In the past

People used to erect towers outside their houses or stores. These towers were used to hang lanterns. The number of lanterns on the tower would be the same as the number of family members. People believed that the brighter the lights of the lanterns that evening, the luckier the family would be. On those days, people tried to make higher poles than their neighbors. These poles held lanterns of every shape and size, such as carp lanterns, watermelon lanterns, ship lanterns, and locust flower lanterns. People also set off fire-crackers made of powder, paper, and string to add more noise and excitement to the party!

Above: South Koreans in the countryside also celebrate this special occasion.

Have you ever seen an elephant this big? It is part of the lantern parade!

Who's Buddha?

In the sixth century B.C., there lived an Indian prince by the name of Siddhartha Gautama. He was a wise man. He found that in order to escape life's misery and achieve **salvation**, one must ignore worldly pleasures. Through meditation and discipline, a person would be able to reach a state of permanent peace and happiness. Such teachings have since been called Buddhism. Buddhism arrived in Korea a long time ago and was widely accepted by the Korean people. In fact, there are more Buddhists than followers of other religions in South Korea. Korean Buddhism also has elements of other religions in it. For example, nearly every Buddhist temple has a chapel containing a **shrine** next to it. The shrine is meant to appease the local mountain spirit, upon whose land the temple has been built.

This giant granite Buddha is a picture of calm and serenity. Buddhist temples usually contain such statues, although they may not be as large as this one!

It is a solemn occasion as these monks circle the pagoda.

Round and round we go

A unique practice is faithfully carried out on Buddha's birthday. Monks and Buddhist devotees walk in circles around pagodas found in the temples. Monks lead the way while the visitors follow. The Buddhists usually carry lanterns or clasp their hands in prayer. All of them chant the praises of Buddha while walking in circles. This practice is called Circling the Pagoda, or *t'apdori* [T'UP-dori]. T'apdori originated as a prayer for a peaceful death and smooth passage to the Buddhist paradise. However, it has become a folk custom over the years. Today, folk songs are played while people circle the pagodas and pray for individual good fortune instead.

Think about this

There are many similarities between Buddha and Jesus. Both could heal the sick and perform miracles. They also preached that the surrender of worldly enjoyments was the way to a better afterlife. Both Jesus and Buddha also had a few wise men witnessing their births! What other famous religious figures can you think of? What did they do to help people?

This woman is "purifying" the Buddha at the temple during the festival. There must be many others waiting in line to do the same.

TAN-O DAY

Tan-O [DHA-no] Day falls on the fifth day of the fifth lunar month. On this day, Koreans pray for good harvests. After prayers, they throw big celebrations like those on New Year's Day. Tan-O activities usually occur outdoors. In villages, people participate in many different activities, such as dancing and group games.

See how skillfully this man is taming the "lion."

A swinging good time!

Playing on a swing is not just for children in South Korea. As a matter of fact, it is one of the favorite amusements of women on Tan-O Day! To make a swing, a long heavy rope is tied to a tree branch on both ends. The rope is then tied to the crossbeam. A woman stands on the rope and swings. Tan-O Day takes place at the beginning of summer. Watching a happy woman in a colorful dress swinging high above the green trees into the blue sky on a summer afternoon is a joy!

Left: On Tan-O Day, people can watch many types of mask dances.

Opposite: Women and girls compete to see who can swing the highest while standing up.

16

Mask dances

On Tan-O Day, South Koreans enjoy exciting mask dramas. People in colorful masks tell a tale through song and dance. One of the mask dances that is popular on Tan-O Day is the Bongsan [PONG-s'han] mask dance. It is performed to dispel evil spirits and pray for crops. Different stories exist within the dance. Some are about lions, while others are about husbands and wives.

In the olden days, the Bongsan mask dance was entertainment for officials in the king's court. Later, it spread to the countryside for the common people to see. Dancers in the villages and towns were usually low-ranking officers in the local governments. They collected money from the rural people to help fund the dance.

Opposite and above: There are many types of mask dances. Each of them have different stories and characters. Don't you think the masks are colorful?

Think about this

Mask dances are important in many cultures of the world. The Hopi, a native American people, wear masks during their ceremonies in spring to summon rain. Also, the Yoruba people of Africa wear wooden masks and perform a dance so that the "mother spirits" will bless them with good health.

CH'USOK DAY

Imagine that you are a farmer. The weather is great. The autumn moon is bright and beautiful. The long hours you spent at the field are rewarded with a plentiful harvest. Your oxen and chickens are growing. With such good things going on, isn't it time to celebrate?

The Koreans certainly think so. Ch'usok [CHOO-soak] Day, or the Harvest Moon Festival, is a day of thanksgiving for the South Koreans. It also happens to be one of their biggest holidays. Ch'usok is celebrated by farmers and city dwellers alike, in appreciation of the good things in their lives.

It's time to whip up a feast

To prepare for the festivities, South Koreans buy wine and fruits such as dates, chestnuts, and **persimmons**. They make food with new grain from the harvests. One of the favorite treats prepared for this holiday is *Kkaegangjong* (KAE-ghang-jung). These are small cakes made from sesame seeds.

In preparation for the feast, this woman spends her time gathering chestnuts.

A legend of kings and cloth weaving

How did Ch'usok start? Legend has it that a long time ago, a Korean king divided his people into two groups. His princesses then led the ladies from each group in a cloth-weaving competition. On the 15th day of the eighth lunar month, the king saw which group had produced more cloth. The group that had done so won the competition, and the defeated group had to prepare a feast to entertain the winners. Then a festival took place. This was how Ch'usok started.

Enjoying the beauty of the moon

At the end of the day, people love to sit back and enjoy the beauty of the full autumn moon. Basking under the rays of the moon, the Koreans read and write poetry. They believe the moon inspires them to be artistic.

On Ch'usok, South Koreans visit their ancestors' grave sites in the mountains. They clear the wild grasses that have grown around the graves since their last visit. Afterward, they pay their respects and offer incense.

21

On Ch'usok, families get up early in the morning. They wear traditional clothes and present prepared foods to their ancestors and family gods in a ceremony at home.

Tortoise play and ox feeding

Many interesting festivities take place during Ch'usok. The activities are usually practiced for good luck or to express thanks for a successful harvest. One activity involves a dance performed by a tortoise!

A huge "tortoise" is made out of corn leaves. Two men get into this costume and dance around. The tortoise visits a farmer's home and collapses after a dance. It then explains to the farmer that it has traveled a long way and needs to be fed. The farmer then offers rice cakes and fruits. The tortoise expresses its gratitude by doing another dance.

The tortoise is the chosen animal for this dance because the Koreans believe that it has **longevity**. It also does not get sick easily. The tortoise play is presented on Ch'usok to ward off evil spirits.

Koreans also have an ox-feeding dance! A man-made ox runs around from house to house, asking for food. It also performs dances to show its thanks.

Two farmers hard at work in their field.

22

Kang-gang-suwollae

On Ch'usok, women in pretty dresses stand in a circle to perform a folk dance. One of them stands in the center and leads the others in a song. These women sing and dance merrily in the circle to a song called "Kang-gang-suwollae" [kang-gang-su-wollae].

Kang-gang-suwollae was actually a smart ploy the Koreans used during wartime. Three centuries ago, when the Japanese invaded Korea, women near the battlefield gathered in circles and sang "Kang-gang-suwollae" around bonfires. This tricked the enemy into thinking there were many defending troops. Since the war, women gather on Ch'usok to sing and dance in commemoration of this practice.

These women are performing the Kang-gang-suwollae for the admiring crowd. They must practice very hard for this occasion!

Think about this
Ch'usok Day is not only a day to remember ancestors. It's also an agricultural festival where farmers celebrate the harvest. Other countries also have agricultural festivals. In Russia, a festival called Sabantui celebrates the completed sowing of crops.

SOKCHONJE RITES

I n the second and eighth months of the lunar calendar, another important person is remembered. He is Confucius, a Chinese **sage** admired for his teachings. On these occasions, Confucius and his students are honored in a ceremony called the Sokchonje [SOAK-kuan-jhe] Rites. The rites take place in a famous university in Seoul, the capital of South Korea.

Divine wine for Confucius

During the ceremony, a dance ritual is performed by people dressed as court officials who offer wine and food to the altar of Confucius. Behind them, eight rows of eight students in traditional costumes dance. They bow left, right, then center. In the first part of the rite, dancers hold flutes and dragon-headed sticks. In the second part, they beat wooden hammers on wooden shields. There are also **incantations** of poems. All these actions are accompanied by traditional music.

This performer is carrying a painted rattle used during the traditional dance of eight rows of eight.

Who was Confucius?

Confucius was a Chinese scholar whose ideas influenced many people. His ideas are called **Confucianism**. Confucius was concerned about improving human relationships. He also wanted to improve the conduct of people in society, and all his teachings were aimed at maintaining peace and harmony between people. Confucius also believed that human relationships, such as those between father and son, were important.

Ever since Confucianism was introduced in Korea, it has greatly influenced Korean life. For example, Koreans have a deep respect for their elders. This is in accordance with the Confucian idea of respect for authority.

Above: Confucius's teachings are very popular in China, and the Sokchonje Rites originated there. It was a ceremony honoring teachers, ancestors, and nature. Now the rites are held only in Korea.

Confucius was a philosopher who recognized the importance of relationships within the family.

THINGS FOR YOU TO DO

South Korean children enjoy many traditional games that are easy to learn and offer hours of fun. Two games South Korean children love are *Jeki* (JAE-ki) and *Kongkee* [KUNG-gee].

Jeki

Jeki is a well-known children's game that is especially popular with boys. This game requires each player to kick a jeki, a homemade shuttlecock, using only the inside or outside of the foot. Whoever kicks the jeki the most times without having it drop on the floor or ground wins!

To make a jeki, you need a big coin (a quarter or some coin that is bigger), tissue paper, and a rubber band. First, wrap the coin in the tissue paper. Then tie the wrapped coin with the rubber band. The wrapped coin should look like a dumpling. Tear the ends of the tissue paper into fine strips and it's done! Kick it around and have hours of fun! Practice kicking the jeki without letting it touch the ground. Then, have a friendly competition with others who like this game, too!

How to play Kongkee

Gather five small stones or pebbles. Start the first four rounds by throwing the stones onto the ground. For the first round, pick up one of the stones. Throw it into the air and grab one of the other stones from the ground. At the same time, catch the stone that is falling down. All this is done with the same hand. Do this with the other stones.

For the second round, pick up two stones from the floor just before you catch the stone in the air. Do this again for the remaining two stones on the ground.

For the third round, throw one stone into the air and collect three stones from the ground. Collect the last stone when you throw one of the stones into the air a second time. For the fourth round, collect all four stones with one swoop while the fifth one is in the air.

Finally, throw all the stones into the air. At the same time, flip your hand. Any stones that fall onto the back of your hand must be thrown up into the air again. Catch them as they fall.

Things to look for in your library

Buddha. Susan L. Roth (Doubleday, 1994).

Chi-Hoon: A Korean Girl. Patricia McMahon (Boyd Mills Press, 1993).

The Long Season of Rain (Edge Books). Helen S. Kim (Henry Holt and Company, 1996).

Older Brother, Younger Brother: A Korean Folktale. Nina Jaffe (Viking Children's, 1996).

The Rabbit's Escape. Suzanne C. Han (Henry Holt & Company, 1995).

Sim Chung and the River Dragon: A Folktale from Korea. Ellen Schecter (Gareth Stevens, 1997).

South Korea: Land of Morning Calm. (video).

Touring Korea. (video).

We Adopted You, Benjamin Koo. Linda W. Girard (Albert Whitman & Company, 1989).

MAKE A FAN

S outh Koreans use fans to cool themselves during summer. In the past, scholars used fans to look dignified, and court ladies used them to cover their faces when they saw men. Fans were also exchanged by provincial governors on Tan-O Day. Today, people still exchange fans as gifts on Tan-O Day and during springtime. Make a fan and cool yourself this summer!

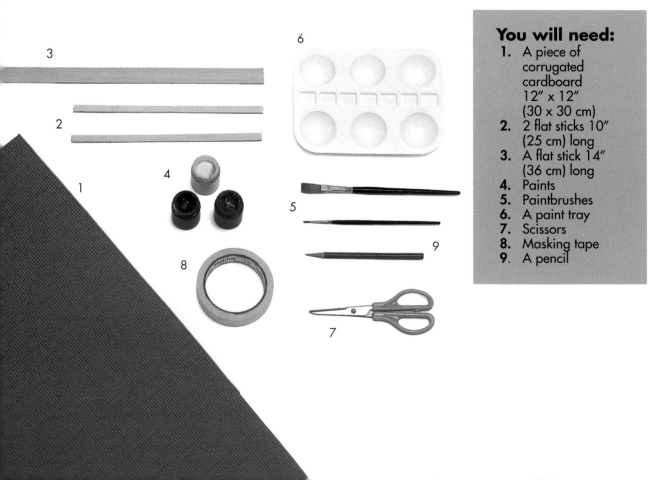

You will need:
1. A piece of corrugated cardboard 12" x 12" (30 x 30 cm)
2. 2 flat sticks 10" (25 cm) long
3. A flat stick 14" (36 cm) long
4. Paints
5. Paintbrushes
6. A paint tray
7. Scissors
8. Masking tape
9. A pencil

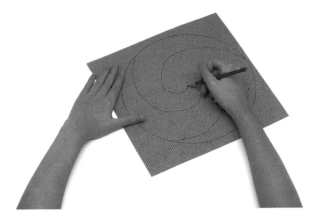

1 Using the pencil, draw a circle on the corrugated cardboard. You can have your own design or follow the design in the picture. Then, cut out the circle with the pair of scissors.

2 Using the masking tape, attach the longest stick onto the cardboard, with only one end sticking out past the circle's outer boundary. Then, attach the two shorter pieces as shown in the picture. The two shorter pieces of stick should cross one another.

3 Finally, paint your fan with many bright colors!

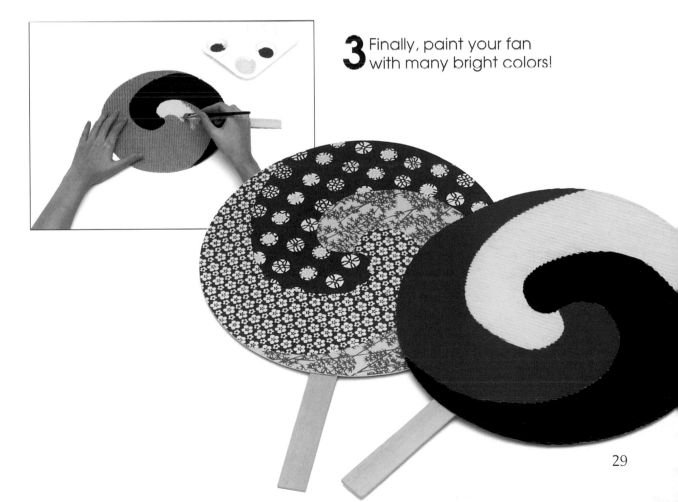

MAKE KKAEGANGJONG

S outh Koreans enjoy sweet cakes and other Korean desserts only on festive occasions. Kkaegangjong is a sesame seed biscuit that is eaten on festive days. Making it can be tricky, but here is a simplified version for you to try!

You will need:

1. Slightly less than ¼ cup (50 grams) black sesame seeds in bowl
2. Slightly less than ¼ cup (50 g) white sesame seeds in bowl
3. ¼ cup (50 g) light brown sugar
4. 8 tablespoons golden syrup
5. Measuring cup
6. Frying pan
7. Saucepan
8. Wooden spoon
9. Measuring spoons

1 In the frying pan, heat the white sesame seeds. Remove the pan from the heat when the sesame seeds start to pop. When the pan has cooled, put the seeds into a bowl. Do the same for the black sesame seeds.

2 Mix the syrup and sugar in a sauce pan. Heat this until the sugar has dissolved. When the mixture has cooled, mix half of this syrup into the bowl containing the black sesame seeds. Mix the other half into the bowl containing the white sesame seeds.

3 Tear off a piece of the white sesame seed paste. Shape it into a flattened, round piece as you see in the picture. When you have finished with the white sesame paste, you can start on the black! Now you have a delicious dessert!

GLOSSARY

adorn, 12 — To make something more beautiful or decorative.
Ceasefire Line, 4 — The border between North Korea and South Korea.
Confucianism, 25 — The ideas of Confucius that emphasizes peace and harmony in human relationships.
filial piety, 9 — A child's gratitude to his or her parents for their care and guidance.
incantations, 24 — The reciting of words that supposedly possess some magical quality.
Korean War, 4 — The war started by North Korea when it tried to unify Korea.
longevity, 22 — Long life.
mock, 11 — Fake; not real.
persimmons, 20 — Orange-colored, sweet fruits that resemble tomatoes.
ravaged, 4 — Almost fully ruined and destroyed.
sage, 24 — A very wise person.
salvation, 14 — An escape or release from the effects of evil.
shrine, 14 — A structure used for religious worship.

INDEX